Sidebox

Catching Out

By
M Bowles

ISBN: 978-1-7331883-2-6

For any inquiries regarding this book please email:
writeaway@fea.net

Contents

Cleaner Than a Hymn

He wiped the alleluia off his hands
And stepped across the chambers of her heart
To build a speckled life
In the sway of the olive ranch
Where the sonnet ran more clean and honest
Than a hymn.

The Tributary Queen

There was a queen
A powerful tributary from distant lands
Who rose and swelled
To cry her bosom into the sea every winter
Bringing with her a mighty legion of felled trees
In the current of her lamentations
But King Neptune was not impressed.

I rule seventy percent of the fifth largest planet
And more grains of sand than stars in the galaxy
He proclaimed and with a flick of his blue robe
Splintered her cellulose army upon the shore
Where humans built them into fragile hopes
And dreamed at night little knowing that the king
Was coming to claim more than the seventy percent.

As for you my queen
The king admonished
You have not the juice to fill my coffers
In the summer I will build a bank of sand
With my big toe to block your rosy hips
And your pelvis will parch away
While your thighs and sighs retreat into dust.

And so he did.

Web Dreams

People have tried to lose their parents
On couches upholstered with their salaries
Spend their adulthood
Scraping the furrow
From their mother's front porch
Now little girls
Lay their Barbie dreams on the train tracks
For a bad comment on the Web.

End Days

Imagine a redwood
Upon seeing the lumberjack
Bending its neck for the axe
A blue whale
Swimming into the harpoon
A duck hovering
Above the blind
Imagine the wind longing for
A room with quiet in every corner
The hunter dreams of
Dropping the deer with a single shot
The sunset looks into the mirror and
Closes her eyes
For the last time.

The Argument

If you haven't heard the sea
Argue with the rain
I have

I made you the sea says
Glaring gray and furrowing his whitecaps
If it weren't for me you'd be just another clear day

Look at you lying there landlocked by the continents
While I have legs to dance across your solar plexus
The rain down poured

But what a waste pirouetting your patter
Water on water
When the almond trees are begging for a drink
I protested from shore

Quiet and run your dog interloper
The wind hissed
Always trying to hurry the Cirrus message along

It was the rainbow who broke things up
Flexing right in God's face
One foot on the Inland Empire
The other igniting the ocean
Just where it falls over the horizon

Two white slivers
Who shouldn't be out in the storm
Turned their bows and raced toward it
To cast their lines
For a pot of gold.

Baptism

They lay the tiny creature of their love
On the green embankment of his conception
Inside a fawn morning
The holy water laying her fingers
On the sacrament of his forehead
As he gazed at the Godparents above
Shedding fond wishes from their evergreen canopy
The blue waving its sky welcome
Behind their branches sway
No clouds dared cross the beam of his vision
And even the harebells rang their tiny pink heads
On the exhale of his breath
There is a sacred stream in all of us
Born from the center of the earth
That wants to run clear and true
Against the flesh of gravity pulling us
Down the slope into the sea
It dislodges the speckled pebble who
Does not heed the brackish tongue
Lives on the creek bottom as pure as the christening
But volunteers for the journey
A polished friend small and round
As the infant's palm.

Poetry Lessons

I set up my easel
In the hall of the masters
They slip out of their frames
One by one
Gather around the white canvas
Show me how to break open the piñata
I ask them to stay
Even the ones who smell like whiskey.

Humming Bird Nest

The shell of your tiny egg
Is as fragile as the rice paper
On the inside of my mother's wrist
Peering through the shades
At the nest you built atop the crown
Of the wind chime
Swaying on the breeze
Of ninety-two years
Dreaming in the thimble
The motor of your buzzing wings
Silent as down
The lint from her dryer
Even a hair from her comb
And her softening heart
Mattress the nest
While my late father watches
From the other side of the screen door
Your little beak raises
A twig of hope
For one more year
Of tiny birds.

The Knowings

In the formless twilight of in-between
When time is holding its breath
When my thoughts have stopped pacing
My breath has found the shallow cup
And my eyes fade into their interior room
The knowings come
Not in words, nor silence
A dark nut falling
Into a quiet river
From a branch on the velvet bank
A small splash
Ahead of the current
In the soft ripple
The Berlin Wall comes down
A woman writes to her twin sister
Of another name
Two spirits waft across the street
Holding hands
For a moment the firefly glows
Its lantern just for me
And only I can know
The names of the fish
Who float up around the bend.

Planet in Handcuffs

Look at you dropping plump grapes from the vine
Into my mouth
Even with wrists bound by barbed wire and coal
It's as it should be
My little planet in handcuffs
Don't pretend the fumes from my hairspray
Offend your delicate ozone
It was you after all who sent your agent
To muss my hair with his southwesterly fingertips
Or complain about the leaking pipes
Under your Montana creek
And the Indians camped out at Wounded Knee
Clear streams and natives are quaint memes
Blown by my jet stream across the prairie
So I can make my investor's meeting by noon
Do you really think you turn by sheer physics?
Do you know nothing about how the sun rises and sets
According to the mechanics of economics?
Or inertia?
The money does not trickle down like they say
It sits on its dead ass
Would languish in the landfill
With the Barbie carcasses and unmatched socks

Were it not for me
Bench-pressing the weight of commerce
Busting my pecs on your behalf I might add
Didn't I give you Earth Day and an electric car?
So a glacier or two have given up and dropped out
A few polar bears drowned
Aren't they supposed to adapt?
Look at me I am happy because the rising tide
Makes Cuba farther from Florida
Survival of the fittest as they say
Quit crying and use the Pacific trash vortex
To build a bridge if you must
I'm just about done with you anyway.

Farm in the Back Yard

If you hadn't had a farm in the back yard
You wouldn't know the affinity of a rooster
For the back of a horse.

If you hadn't had a farm in the back yard
You wouldn't have seen him
Flap onto the chestnut haunches
Sprint his bantam feet
Along the sway of the back.

If you hadn't had a farm in the back yard
You wouldn't have known the big gelding
Hanging his head over the side fence
Turning his ears to your pitchfork
And gossip with the neighbors on the other side.

If you hadn't had a farm in the back yard
You wouldn't have seen the rooster
Scuttle up the staircase of the red mane
And drop his roost a horse-hair hat
Lording down on the dusty paddock.

If you hadn't had a farm in the back yard
You wouldn't have known the press of the city
Just down the street
Pawing and exhaling monoxide and grease
Launching winged spears into the altitude
To roar the rooster back into the coop
And remind you
That a farm in the back yard of a city
Is only a feathery dream.

Night Snores

I paddled up the river of snores
Through the pink rainforest of my nostril
The portage across the parched lakebed
Of my pallet was tough
Going over the fall of my throat
The deep rumbling tsunami
Almost capsized my little craft
But with masterful strokes
I found refuge on the high ground
Of the lump where my lover
Kicked me out of bed.

Bluebird Canyon

Let us hunt for sacred things
Above the walking hills
Bits of birdsong in the dead twigs
Nests cradling on the breeze
Crows commuting to the wire
Kestrel chicks hover
The last fingers of sun
Firelight a burnished slope
And always the canyon
Sentinel, arms folded to the sea

Catching Out: Mt. Whitney

He went to fetch his brother at the top of the mount
Highest in the lower forty
Bristlecone Pine below gasping for oxygen
Could only use binoculars
To admire the granite peak
All forehead and thin air
But the snowpack stepped a frosty foot
Across his way
Sent him back down the mountain
Only nineteen
Hitching the back seat of a VW bus
Along the spine of the I-10
Where the vapors hula hoop
The asphalt prairies of El Paso
And he heard his brother's voice when the
Train whistle ricocheted
Its call to the polished track
Broken rock back-slid his Vibram soled assault
Of the box car gathering to a gallop
Set his life's reach on the open slider, the pushup and high jump

He'd never mastered in physical education but did
In one leap of fear above the steel piranhas
Of the wheels gnashing below
Smacked his scraped resolution on the high platform
With no tears or forgiveness on his panting bruised back
The platform so high for so low in the lower forty.

Catching Out: Train Hopping

His mother's kitchen wrapped him in the oven mitt
Of warm banana bread
Settling his bruises against the grid of cardboard
Swaying as neat as the squares on a calendar
Empty of the dates in his mind that saw
He had never called home
Rattling further south of caring
To fetch his brother
But for the poison spiders the size
Of the candy bars in his empty backpack
The man with the black suit coat
Who stepped from behind the banana boxes
Told him and squashed the hairy creature
Just getting to know his forearm
Where he crept into the far corner
Of exhaustion

There was nothing to rob him of but his mission
And he was beyond fear
Of the man whose face grew from the totem
Of the thunderbird named Bob.

Catching Out: Switched

His lurching soul was glad for
The crossties flat-sevening the wheels
In the syncopated jazz of his new fast forward
And the banana boxes
With the air holes onto his ripening
Next minute
The dust mote genies seducing
The sun through the crack in the door
And his head swaying
At the end of his neck
Until the motion
Fell onto its knees
Before the brakes
Decoupled his destination
From the future of his next move
And the line stopped its resolve
While the diesel engines made their getaway
Leaving a chain of box cars and flat beds
A mile long without pursuit
And the gold syrup prairie spilled across
The table of nowhere
Only the grin

Of wind bowing the desolate grass in a pageant
Pointing to his next move
A leap into the hope of his boots
Towards the big bosomed horizon
Blocked hard by the grip on his shoulder
The shake of the totem head
She'll bleach your bones in her cleavage
With no mal intent
Stay in the shade of your precinct
The track vibrates with the engines
Hastening to couple the destination of your brother
And they sat to their near death for 36 hours
In God's hot breath
Though death never crossed his mind.

Catching Out: New Orleans

A panhandler plies his sainthood
Three rungs down
By squeezing the juice from strangers
Unlike a gentleman of the rails like Bob
Who reveled in his own resources
Dipping a comb in a pocketed jar of water
Run through his hair
When the time called for a leap of faith
Jump Bob said and jumped
A fine Cherokee from Oklahoma
Who could teach a nineteen-year-old to break
The void above the rushing ground
Roll on his fear
Dust the speck of dirt from his suit coat
Just a mile north of the city
Where a man could brew
A mean cup of Joe through a pair of women's hose
And coffee grounds dredged
From the dumpster fire in a soup can of water
Near the center of New Orleans
Where he went to fetch his brother
Which is where the new engines took them
The kindness brewing in the bowl of gumbo

Through the screen door back step of the club
Where he lost his heart to jazz
And almost the boots off his exhaustion
In the night
To the panhandlers in the park
Who would have just as soon slit his throat
Were it not for Bob sitting vigil
Turning him to the bus station where he found
A locker and a day job building fences
And enough change to call his mother
Although he never had fetched his brother.

Catching Out: End of the Tunnel

———————

Only after he had lived
With his bare feet on the slippery rocks
Finding some purchase
On the foothold of his journey
As the years crept their moss underfoot
And he stopped visiting his brother's grave
Under the California Oak behind the church
Floated his wife's ashes of forty years
Along the alpine pool
Where they skinny-dipped their young love
Into three fine children who each
Crested Whitney of their own right
Only when what was left of their earthly union
Had swirled into the clitter-clatter
Of the runaway creek dead set on the sea
Did he hear the far-off whistle of the freight train
Entering the tunnel at the top of the grade
And in an instant of the breeze catching its breath

The polished track vibrated in his veins
The totem face rose above the black suitcoat
So many revolutions of the wheels ago
Only then did he see
Bob was the brother sent to fetch him.

Shut Out

The tide pools will not
Speak to me
Their mouths are filled with sand
The crabs have been abducted by the sea
Or found a condo on the land.

Late Valentine

Our hands have avoided
Paper jams
Our bodies' friction
With little wear
Our mouths
Make words that walk in
Each other's sentences
You woke me in the middle of the night
To look at the moon
Gasping up from the purple hill
Then breast-stroking across the sky.

Tribal Bones

Can the Lakota Sioux out-race
The serpent
From Standing Rock to Washington
On teenage feet?
A prophecy to deliver:
The Black Snake of earth's destruction
Slithers up the hill.

It was too heavy for the bones
Of the tribe elders to carry,
The hunter gatherers, marched
From earth's womb
Swaddled in scarlet fever,
Fortified with fire water.

From the bottle of despair
They fanned the council fire
Passed the sacred pipe
The granite of earth's plight
To the ragged youth.

As the parents of freedom
What wisdom can we share?

The lung bartered for a pot of oil?
A vote bought with Fahrenheit
Causing flesh to spoil?
The carcasses of the species
Under our command?

The parents of freedom,
We have abdicated our role,
Hidden the bloody knife
Under the couch of comfort.

Slack Tide

Fog hangs loops of gauze
The bow lost in its weave
The motor's throat echoes back
Inside the ocean ghost cove
May as well shut it down
You are stuck in the swamp of slack tide.

Thirteen miles from your home shore
And thirteen to the Island's port
One deck-shoe on the threshold
One deck-shoe out the door
No forward and no back
Only slack tide.

Even the experts of navigation
Are falling from the sky
The flock of exhausted birds
Drops to your fly bridge
No one out-flies the fog.

Forget the technology
That is your crutch
The dim-witted radar
The GPS, the depth finder
By the time they sound the alarm
The looming container ship
Will have swallowed your minnow.

You are in slack tide
Ring the fog bell
Do you remember how to pray?

Naked Lake

Lover, come across the inlet
Where the shallows will worship your feet
Bring your tired smile
To the hammock of these worried breasts
Time could not out-swim
The fringed shoreline of our desire
Here on the blind sand
Where the redwood leans in
Let us go into the naked lake
And drop a pebble into the pool.

Smallest Sparrow

People listen to a fallow master
Because it is easy
They follow a shepherd
Who promises to protect them from the wolf
He has drawn always salivating just under the bed
I am the seamstress tailoring the yellow Protea
In my front garden
A burst of yellow pin cushions
Their heads open as cotton
Then grow orange tips
Arrows who point out spring
A hawk carving above
Only sees the season of his hunger
And the ground with no argument
Crows peck at his eyes
To spare their chicks to eat other chicks
Our sky is but a blue lesson
That the wind belongs to
Even the smallest sparrow.

The Great Die Off

These are polarizing times
But not for the polar bear
He is already sunk
On an ice cube sighing into the
Martini of the human morass
Who needs polar bears? Or tigers?
Or elephants save for their ivory?
What is the great die-off but another
Shade drawn
On closing time at happy hour
For the ocean, the jungle
Where the animated exodus
Snarls at your Tyrannosaurus Rex
And your human number is called into
The third ring of the circus
Stare into the plastic cup and know
You are just another
Empty straw in the fast-food doom
Of your existence.

April O'Neill

You can climb on your lover's shoulders
To rescue the red hen roosting in the tree
Against the possum in the branch above
Stagger up the dust in the paddock
As she flaps her wings
In the face of your good intentions
Pecks your hand upon the brown egg
Still warm from her body
You can get on your knees
To flick her grubs
From the fresh earth with your trowel
She hovers and pecks at your hip
Comes when you call her turtle superhero name
Then dies feet-up in her coop.

Cannabis Collective

If you want to see
Generations in harmony
Then get thee
To the nearest dispensary.

Blue Trolley

The blue trolley circles
Every forty minutes
But never arrives
Bumping where the tree roots rear up the road
Boarding others at the stop
A wet spaniel
Who shivers under the bench
An old woman clacking her dentures in tongues
While the shaman clears us
With burning sage and eagle feather
Turning off our destiny
To drop me at the weeping well
Where pennies fall like eyes
From the change machine.

Hopeless Side of the Waves

I am walking on
The hopeless side of the waves
Recovering drug addicts
On beach chairs
Their healer delivers a sermon
Under an umbrella
Their money and their relapses
Locked down in his cooler.

Men with empty backpacks
Jeer at the one
Doing clumsy tricks on a skateboard
A broken piece of menace
Under the park bench.

The tourists rode home on summer
The seagulls have given up
On sand crabs
Huddle on forlorn breasts
With no Cheeto.

I could take off my clothes
Swim through the waves
To the other side
Where the sea is kind and pure
But the water is too cold.

Overheated Earth

Forgive us innocents, you who have reaped
The grapes we have been fermenting into an overheated earth
On the boy, only fourteen who can't outrun
The decades of bad decisions that
Burn him to death by the elderly couple who die in the garage of our
Impasse smoke succumbs the wife
In her husband's arms
Beneath the backyard pool of our squabbles
Frayed firefighters heft the over-consumption of generations
Dependent on black greed bubbling up
From deep in the earth we seek to quench
With 747's and tankers, jet streams of fire retardant
Red as the blood charred in your veins you kindred
Bodies we inhale your smoke into
Our lungs cry your embers the bill
Has come due at the five-star restaurant
In a singed envelope at the corner of the table where we
Turned our sacred national mouth
From the lips of Paris CPR for the common breath the bill

Has come due and if our species is no longer
Here to pay it the earth will still be here to collect our generation
Is no longer innocent the alarm has sounded put down
Your Bibles and your smart phones and rain down the
Wrath on the roof of Congress we are no longer innocent.

May We Be Fools

___

May we be fools enough to befriend
The little birds who pull up to the
Twig at our rooftop
To share their secrets.

May we be open to the
First names
Of the lizards who gather up
The summer light
On our garage walls.

May we find time
To free the butterfly wing
From the sticky
Web of autumn
Under our carport.

I am silly to tell the bent elm
That his brown leaves
Fall from the mouth of my youth
Onto our front lawn.

Or lecture the stairs
To the atrium
About the bending
Of knees.

You and me, my love
Sunbathing in the naked side yard
We will stretch our devotion
Over the wound of time.

Muse is Coming

My muse is coming to town honey
No wine or fucking tonight
Only keyboards banging each other
Until the morning light.

Brown Bird

I heard of a girl who was afraid of birds
Perhaps she was a worm in a previous life
They fly in from the spirit world
With breasts of pussy willow
Yellow messages on their beaks
A little brown one hopping through the atrium
The bright eye of the ninety-six-year-old architect
Who died with his scotch in the sage armchair
Inspecting the wall we brought down
To invoke the green-eyed hill
The tap of his twigged feet
Through my bedroom fever down the hall
Seven days I heard him pass
Until the fever broke
Then taking wing for home.

Fire Season

Winds bring their burning breath
From the south
Their brittle flute
Cracks skin into scales
Bows cedars into dust
Red fire flags point in the canyon
The poison core parches my mouth
A spark could hop in the night
Sleep paces on the rooftop
Our fears are in a pile by the door
The engine runs in the garage
The yellow sign warns
There is only one way out.

Purple Grief

The sea urchins are
Gone, burrowed their purple grief
Into the tide rock.

Playa Gift Economy

I washed feet in the desert
It was a party all right
Soaked those little puppies in a dishpan
Then scrubbed them pink and bright.

Took a shot of tequila
Gave them a good massage
Rubbed in a healing foot balm
Heard stories in a great barrage.

They stretched out their fate
Into the palm of my lap
Followed the plight of Afghanistan
On the journalist's map.

Learned how the transgender rocket scientist
Made jet engines sing
How the young Ethiopian saved
The people's bread from a warlord king.

So press the Nazarene spot
Just below the big toe
And your mystic fingers will uncover
The everlasting sole.

Polished Stone

What is this polished stone
You brought to me
In the palm of your calloused soul
From the clear river-bottom of a tributary
Beyond mine but so close to the bank
I knew its oval shape and brown speckle
As if I had smoothed it with my current
Before it left its place
Where the trout waits for the fly
In the shade below the riffles
And the waters fray and trickle close
On their barefoot path
Resisting
Resisting
Until the eyes bubbling on the surface
The ones who calculate the clear deeps
And know when it is time for the stone
To let go and flow to the sea.

The Others

_____

The others crouched on the pavement
And talked of the morning's take
A gulp of coffee a wedge of breakfast burrito
And what might happen to them, the unwanted
The city says it is a sanctuary, cardboard beds
And the crunch of needles underfoot
Do I dare speak of sanctuary to the woman
Railing against the man wailing
And wedges of burrito from the trash?
Let us find a washed corner you and I
Where we will collect words in the hat
Leave the unwanted
To sleep under the hardened stars
Spitting a glow
That might be dead a hundred years ago
The slope of liberty slides into the tomb.

Walking Hills

I live in the walking hills
Their noses point to the sea
The slide of their dirt feet
Eager for the shore.

Cason and retaining wall
Strain to their intent
Broken beams and sewage lines
And foundations of human will
Follow in their wake.

They bend their knees
And the lady in the white nightgown
Rushes down
Trailing her house behind.

I live in the walking hills.
I see the crows feet growing
In the cement of my front landing
We are all walking towards the sea.

Executive Extinction

Retired oil company executives
Are washing up in glass houses
Overlooking the oceans they polluted
Throw not a rock through their window
Ye of the combustible metal animal
Guzzling their gas and galloping
Your economy on the bodies
Of lost dinosaurs
Dying their carbon extinction.

Silver King Farewell

On the pillow of my dream
Our family gathered in a room
Of mahogany horizontals
Even the children
Blowing smoke through the open window
Gray vespers into the night…
In the morning I heard over coffee
That you had almost sunk
Were being dismantled
We rushed our dismay to the boat docks
Approached the blue dumpster with dread
Found your treasure scattered in the coffin
The violation of your teak deck,
Tarnished running light
Once loved to a sheen when you
Were under our watch
The curtain sewn, lines rolled
Into clean marlinspikes
By little hands now fully grown
Was it your spirit who willed our eyes to the water?
Tethered to the dock, your carcass

No more than the skeleton of a whale
But your still proud bow
Curved up like an offering
In your sides I recognized the mahogany horizontals
Where our family had gathered in my sleep
Exhaling our seafaring memories
Through your portholes
For the stars to keep.

Groom Story

He waved the present back down the driveway
And went to rescue his future
On the side of the freeway
In a hundred- and six-degrees Fahrenheit
That fried the egg of the engine block
So only the tow truck he called
Could drag the carcass down the ramp
Of his new love
Onto the beach where the lightening hurled
A bolt at the rehearsal dinner
While rain accepted the invitation they had
Hand pressed on cotton stock
Guests two-stepping the paper parasols
Into umbrellas
Though the sun wrung out in time
For the Pacific to witness the ceremony
As the rainbow smiled into the photographer's lens
Above his shoulder and what was he to do
With all those wedding photos
Into the album of tiny teeth
Under the tooth fairy pillow
His future sizzling spit
On the side of the hundred and six degree
Fahrenheit freeway.

Mars Puppy

Hello you big red cabbage
Mars in the southern sky
Mouthing above the August
Humid on my naked
Peeing of the puppy in the sleeping hours
When the moon slides cool
As a school bus across the ridge
Did the orange comb-over of your fury
Propel the Nazis boys from their bedroom war games
Onto the streets of the brown shirts
Buttons torn from purpose
What could they have made before
We infatuated with all things cheap?
Let the storks take them by the nape of their hate
Deliver them to their twin bonfire in the east
My puppy pees unsteady legs on the grass
His eyes only fill with love
And morning warm tongue
I am naked in the moon.

Spider Web

Spider, weaving your web
Where I walk by
Do not get in the way of a human head
If you expect to catch a fly.

Baby Mammal Fish

Little baby leviathan
Bouncing on the knee of the flatbed
You little mammal fish
Red and blue caution lights of the police car
Flashing on the iridescent flukes of your tail
Almost touching the pavement
From out of your canvas shroud
Just a little baby not even a minnow tear drop
In the sob fest of the sea
Did you even get your first breath
Or did the weight of sorrow
Wrap your umbilical cord around its own grief
Where was your mother
Did she abandon you for the surface
To chase off a boat full of oglers
Smothering your first breath
Or were you just a still-born dream
Where the wave wept you onto the sand
The gleam of my front bumper
Not as luminous as your lifeless tail
Wending the canyon funeral
Up the drive where they rescue baby sea lions
But not a baby whale.

Artificial Evolution

Artificial intelligence keeps
An ever-learning plan
Outpacing the human brain
Within the digital clan.

Are we the human race
The first creature to decide
Our evolutionary path
Without a groom or bride.

Emboldened by our accomplishments
We push the outside in
To create ourselves as cyborgs
For electronics the second skin.

Today as I drove down the hill
Two boys stood ready for school
One on each side of the street
Ear-budded up and cool.

Not a conversation to be had
Or even a friendly shove
Each in their separate world
Slaves to the digital cloud above.

Great scientists and thinkers
Warn of Prometheus unbound
I think he has already arrived
And brought fire without a sound.

Jerusalem Cricket

I think of the Jerusalem cricket
Who pedals into the atrium on his trike
I will not squash him though he is hairy
And his fangs pierce the skin.

The woman cradles her conference call
And doodles
With hush colored pens
While the parking garage listens in.

The yacht slides like midnight
Through the moorings
Where boats slumber without the moon
Pivots on her satin shoes
We fend her off on the port stern.

The grapefruit falls velvet plush
Onto the lawn outside my bedroom
The cricket escapes under the Eucalyptus
In the beam of the flashlight.

Sand of Worry

At dusk uneasiness and foreboding arrive
The surf lingers through a rock shelf
By night the tide pools are underwater
The crab tumbled out to sea
With claw and things of sorrow
Which in the morning will be buried under the sand.

Dinosaurs Grew Wings

Dinosaurs grew wings
So eagles and sparrows
Could dart above the great extinction
The grove of programmers
Sprout code in a race
Against the dark foliage of human nature
And the tar pit of power
Will the artificials be kind
When we are but fossils?

The Least Among Us

You are the dirty leaves
Of that city, collecting in corners,
Driven off the branches by the great fall.

We sweep you from turned-away emergency rooms
Where the pavement serves
As mental health facility, rehab and career arc.

You hunt with outstretched hands
Into soft-spoken moments when we recognize in you
The hungry Savior
But there are so many Saviors
You trip us when we are just trying to get to the camera store.

I try to keep my eyes up so I cannot see that you are really me
But when yours' met mine, I saw how warm they were
For such a frigid night.

Cat in the Box

Relax my child
Though the cat in the box is in short supply
Dead or alive
Only the computers know in their freezing baths
The sunbathing sea lion
Charges the dog on the sand
Does not know they are cousins
And the ocean mother calls him back
While an unmarked envelope lands on the driveway
In the middle of the night
We will not open it
Come into the wilderness
Where the truth runs cleaner than the wind
Lay yourself on the soft earth
Where we have smoothed you
A bed beneath the redwood
Although we will fade into the forest
Your existence bends towards itself
At the edge of the meadow
Where all questions will be answered
For you hold them all
Beneath the outline of your dreaming face.

Hillside Awakening

New tracks upon our hillside go
New fingers pull the weeds
A coyote cry upon the hill
Brings rabbits into heed.

New children in the tree house swing
Growing up with each new rung
And still the restless fall returns
Before the cool has sung.

Extinction

You balance on the tide rock,
The ocean arches its blue back to you
Sprays crowns of foam
But you are typing a tweet.

Walking on the beach
The waves sing to you
But you are wearing ear buds.

We stand at the fulcrum of miracles.
The generous meadow in June
The stream below the hotpots
The peaks above the clouds.
But we do not see the harebell
Crushed beneath our cross-trainer
The flash of the brown trout in the shadow
The spray of the blue whale sounding
In the faceless mouth of your smart phone.

The glacier faints into the ocean
And the Atlantic bubbles up in the lawn in Miami Beach.
The polar bear's lungs fill with seawater
While our missiles flex their biceps
The user interface does not show
That flesh will be burned from the bone.

The oracles of fossil fuel decree
That the earth has endured many changes
Pliocene, ice age, plate tectonics, volcanic eruptions
It will carry on, they proclaim
They are right
The earth will continue her twirling dance around the sun
It is the creatures of the meadows, the streams, and Instagram
Who will not.

End of the Troubles

There is no light at the end of the troubles
Only right now, right here, just you
If it's too dark
Find the moonlight in the whites of your eyes
The North Star on the gleam of your teeth
The aurora from the calcium in your bones.

Orange Cat

Our future is the orange cat
I carried in my arms like a newborn baby
You hurrying to close up
The back of the house
The open space where the breeze likes to pass
From the green canyon
Me worrying about buttering her paws
So she will find home
While the coyotes come down from the hills
To pace below the balcony.

El Nino Magic

It was the bad ass El Nino
Who brought the green tufts,
Not the polarized lens
Of dark glasses.

Who shed the shy water
Receding against the brush,
Not the glint of mirage
In the driver's eye.

Who lured the dragonfly to survey
Terrain where no insect
Could have made a living,
Not the open window
Of a Westfalia van.

Who coaxed the wild horses
Over the ridge
To bare their teeth against the grass,
Not the cowboy from Reno.

It was the clouds touring
Across the big-hearted sky
Who drenched new life
Into these barren badlands.

Fallen Leaves

Just because you plant
A tree that won't weep
Doesn't mean your neighbor won't
And you spend the rest of your life
Raking up his tears.

Friendship Dishwater

How long have we washed each other's china
Known the easy move to the fill the basin
Find the plastic dish soap under the sink
With bubbles not words
The deep waters of friendship
Under the running faucet of the parent's
Fortieth wedding anniversary
The baptism and graduation
Before the sudden funeral of your father
Then your mother where the aunties nudged
Me away
We know the crystal pitcher bursts
When the rinse water is too hot
And the everyday glasses
Can overload the dishwasher
Oh how the dishtowels dry on the line
As the afternoon revolves around the sun
Yet there you are at the sink
When the wedding wishers overflow the brunch
And we laugh as I flip pancakes at the steaming griddle.

Beyond the Shore Break

In this dog-eat-dog world
The blond retriever from the shelter
Heaves the wisdom
Of seven years to every one of earth's rotation
Onto the sand
Lowers her groaning joints
To groom the puppy so full of teeth and himself
Beyond the shore break
The dolphins sing their injured
Into the calm waters
The whale folds the diver
Under its fin to protect her from the shark
While the great sapient spurns the Bastille
Leaves the summit and the planet
In a hot rage.

Leonardo

The quarrelsome bantam rooster
With the iridescent red and purple plumes
Struts between pride and pride
Not to himself the fertilizer of eggs
I, who am to myself a carrier of fertile eggs
One at a time through the months
Waited for the birth of the three
Carried the rooster in the dark of night
In the back of a truck with the lights off
To empty him across the road
Into a farmyard of ripe hens.

Octopus: Mr. Eight Arms

How have you landed here my wise friend
Plated among the parsley and lemon?
Your salty mind and crafty legs fried to a crisp
In the pan
The gas burning its dominion
Over your intellect outpacing the whale
And many blood cousins I know
The coconut you take up in your eight arms
To tiptoe across the submerged sand
Then architect a safe shelter
Your heroic escapes from the laboratory aquariums
Worthy of a blockbuster
Your passion and family history
Sizzled into a French fry
They pass your plate but not the stories
The extra-terrestrials who may have abandoned you here
No DNA upon those roiling fingerprints
Only the sweet of your flesh against our barbarous lips
How do we choose those smart brains to sacrifice for the appetizer?
Even my leather belt had a mother.

Give Me Back the Twilight

Give me back the twilight
It's the blanket for my soul
The sun conducts the birdsong
Into a murmur low.

The vacant day turns her back
And slips into the shade
The sky drops a pink negligee
Onto the ocean's suede.

Clouds stretch their sooty arms
To warrior back the dark
As the breeze holds its breath
And the hill flairs a last green spark.

I am the furred creature
Charmed by your gentle spell
Lifted from my earthy burrow
To dream your silk lapel.

And as the first star conspires
To pull the ebony scroll
Give me back the twilight
It's the blanket for my soul.

Street Corner Homeless

_____

We will step over
Your homelessness
On the street corner
But do not lay it
Down on our front
Succulent garden.

Eternal Earth

Hello you cypherous peaks
I am back
Lured by your eternal ways
The yellow stripe of the highway
Our umbilical cord.

Which if you is responsible for
The lava tangoing on black feet
Across the sage?
The small guy with the red rounded shoulders
At the top of the rise
Or the little sister we passed an hour ago?

You could shatter a missile
With the enamel of your teeth.
Our soft-shelled endeavors.

Which one of you created the earth?
You will not tell me, will you.

First Flight of the Cooper Hawk

How lopsided your first flight
Plummeting from the down of your mother's attention
The see-saw of gravity
Laughing up from the field
Until you find the gyroscope of your wingspan
And a solid fence that will answer
The first yawn of talons
Old enough to squeeze
The life from a mouse
Where you cling as if your life depended on the strength
Of its cellulose resolve
The breeze fussing the speckled dandelion of your breast
While you play fierce
Resisting the call of your father to the fragile branch
Where he would feed you a young lizard.

I should like to fly on new wings
With all the checkered feathers of hope
And beak as yellow as the morning
Hunting the wind
To lift me in its sacred circle
With my desire sharp-eyed
On all the small wakings of the canyon.

I have heard the cry of the hawk
How dawn flowed through your shadow
Sending even the smallest ant back into its hole
I watch, my feet heavy on the earth
Your dominion over the nest
And the blue trajectory of your freedom.

Apartment Above the Garage

When I found the landing
You lifted a cup filled with sun
We sorted out the laundry key
And walked the soup tureen
With our future
Into the apartment above the garage.

Pink Gorilla

The beast rises at midnight
To share her bare breast on the Playa
Dragging her knuckles through the dust
Go Go dancers obey the deep base
Through misted chain curtains
A pink gorilla three stories high
Sways on his sticks
His handler leaps to the stage
To dance like a primate.

Grandfather Time

My grandfather wound his future
With a brass key
Christened the mechanism of time
Laid out on the garage workbench
Tiny springs and screws spilling from
The red tobacco can
With the royal visage
How could I know the import of his hour
With the time clacking its teeth
On every wall of the house he shared
With my grandmother
How could the tiny pendulums
Of the little bird houses
Out wag the serious schoolroom cadence?
They clap their hands in the same dance with the numbers
Though their choreography was a mystery to me
A grandchild running through the empty field
Dollar bill in my hand for the fast-food taco
My father would never allow
Slicing my foot on the jagged tip of my future
How could any of us know that the chimes and cuckoos
Would submerge into the worship of the smart phone
Who demands our time

And knows our secrets
The chimes and cuckoos who chorused the crescendo
Of my weekend sleepover
And that my grandfather gave to every guest
Until the walls were bare
And he was free to go.

Café Souffle

Orphan child, queen of the kitchen
Whirring of the mixer
Wets the mouths of the faithful
Murmuring silk fine wine
Simple ambiance
Forty years on your feet
Feeding the appetites of the city
Frail foam rising in the bowl
Raised in a French covenant
The breeze of secret recipes
Against your ear
The last gasp of your mother in childbirth
Where was your father
Or are you a devil's child?
What do you think about an ocean away
As you whisk the eggs luscious
Two loyal waiters flourish
Hot and steaming white tablecloths
Gruyere, leek, chanterelle, lobster, chocolate, lemon
Sometimes a hundred a night forty years
Only you in the kitchen
And a man to wash the dish
Reverent we wait to receive the sacrament

What is the cipher bubble above your head
As you conjure the eggs into air?
I only know you from the
Rich brown crust and airy truth that owns me back
Was the nun who taught you
On the cold floor of the convent kitchen kind?
Did she place the warm hope of
Your dead mother on your shoulder as you
Leaned over the bowl?
From what I know of convents I fear not
Your kitchen corner is more sacred
Than a church
Your soufflés rise higher than heaven.

Falcon in the Field

I have sent my falcon out into the field
Look at the rabbit he has laid at your need
Do you not know you are hungry?
Will you let the grass grow to your waist
The carcass rot
And the falcon and I pass into the woods
Leaving only these feathers?

In the Salon

Beneath the ice
The river has a warm throat
She wants to dip in the sea
The woman with the Library of Congress on her head in foil
Wants to know where the beach went
While she was living in Texas
There is no longer a place for the lounge chairs at the hotel
We wear matching black robes
But are we even?
Is the masque to bring the bright back to my brunette
But a light show?
The pelican drops from the pink morning formation
And the sea will return the shore
In its own good time.

Tahoe

I only asked for the key to the laundry room
Not your heart
From the woman who read the future in the ice cubes
Of your glass as it hit the table
And my footsteps on the stairs of the
Chestnut horse we named under the snowfall
Where the balloon bumped its head at you from the high rafters
As you tried to land it with your sweatshirt
Flung beneath
My father's frown
We were witnesses to our wedding
Photographers and musicians
And the golden Eagle who officiated
From the highest branch of the white fir tree.

New Tenants

_____

Dial 911
My new tenants in the Ficus
Are murderers
Felons from the nest
Sharp talon and beak
Savages with a
Wingspan that cuts
The song from the sky
Before the nuthatch
Even knows
He has died mid-flight.

No Clear Path

I follow my shadow along the beach
It looks like it knows where it is going
On legs of pulled taffy
The fall light flanks in low
Beams the waves into crystal
It does not guide me
There is no clear path through the sand
Only a cosmos of indifferent grains
Reshaped each night by the tide
And confused by a tangle of tracks
If the savior had walked here
His footprints have been trampled
On the return trip my shadow
Hunkers down behind
The mathematician works in the sandwich shop
Solves the equations of the universe on break
The adjunct professor meets her Johns on weekends
To cover the rent
I stagger through the sand.

Whichever Way

Whichever way, the shallow path
With the telephone wires asking to
Be buried under the asphalt
Whichever way, the shingled birdhouse
Where we can trade books
Like goodwill behind the glass
Where walkers look into the side yard
As young trees press new taproots against
The dry season and fire pants
Just over the hill
I hear the thirst of the coyotes
Who come down to lap
From my neighbor's fountain
The scrub oak plant their feet and know
That California was always a desert
The wagon trains are leaving for the north
As the cars circle the parking lots
Where there are no spaces
And the apartments rise on their hind legs
To balance on the colored ball
The ring-leader cracks the whip
What can we do but check the blind spot
And love our cars into the passing lane.

Inherited Lily

I left my thought in the alley
Crouching behind the back gate
In the amble of twilight
An inherited lily
Sly root through plastic bag
Thriving up the hum of pavement
Standing down firecrackers
And summer boys
Raving weed whacker
The mover's tread
Tougher than a light post
The leaves reboot
And blaze their raiment
Find new legs
In another bed
In another house
In another time.

Metamorph

Six months after his father passed away
He could not cross a bridge
In a car or on foot
On the way home from the
Memorial when his mother died
He pulled over and vomited
His childhood
On the side of the freeway.

Pedestrian Down

One siren cannot save the city
Rattling the chopsticks of your ears
Banging its head against the high rise.

The fire devoured the earthquake.

Who told the crosser his bone mass
Could out macho the lower lip of a bus?
The driver sobs on the curb
His boss just wants an affidavit
We stop to unnerve our hands
But the catastrophe gives us the finger
From the passing lane.

Global Warming

The sister in the doctoral program
Presided her clipboard
Over the empty swimming pool
Filled with animals
Chickens nuzzled the soft mouth of
The lion's mane
And the cougar forgave the mountain biker
He had just devoured
Within the perimeters of civilization
Unhinged
Beneath the watch of the frozen peak
Thawing
Joints loosening
Flowing their afterbirth into the sea
Rising to reclaim what always
Was hers.

Tent of Civilization

There you are
Asleep on the sand
Halfway in an unzipped tent
Hiding out from the handcuffs
Of the homeless shelter
And overnight camping codes.

Your minnow cousin down the beach
Imprisoned by the tide
In a rock aquarium
Paddling circles
Above a sentinel of anemone
And hermit crabs.

You rose from the sea
Her fins became your arms
Her tail your legs
And no zipper will maroon you
In the tent of civilization.

You will forage your food
From the dumpster and the
Goodness of a passerby
She will escape only when
The moon and the tide connive
To set her free.

Barefoot on the Moon

The universe has a mouth
And it wants to speak to you
From the whale shimmering
Her wake of stardust
Trailing the ancient
Songs of the ocean through
The unknown value of a comet
Studded with precious metals
Un-mined by the brazen astronauts
Who know how to break gravity
With the hammer of their daring
Where my dreams can take me
Weightless from explosions of jet fuel
And towers turning to the earth
The fragile engines of man's ambitions
Jettison to bang their heads
On the laws of physics
While I walk barefoot on the moon.

Ghost of Bad Decisions

The damned ghost of bad decisions
Wearing the white bed sheet
Is staring me down again
From his cut-out eyes
His maternal cousin
The ghost of decisions past
Is groping the ghost of decisions future
In the closet of indecision.

Orange Groves for Plough Shares

———————

There was a backyard gate
That swung into a magic grove
Of forts and deep blue peacocks
Caretakers on horseback
Pulling the sun over their shoulders
To summon green buds from the branch
Until the bulldozers ordered
The oranges to sacrifice their juice
For your blood lust --
Missile sheathes turning on the lathe
And the perspiration of machines
Smelling of medals and power
Tipping the globe on its axis
And into your laps
Looping the cable of your will
Around the neck of history
Even the moon was yours
Smirking within reach through the
Upside down grove
Roots rising like the claws of dead chickens
Goodbye fruit fights

Vivid birds on the morning lawn
The blossoms sharing their sweetness
With the evening air
Only dust rising an apparition
My mother drew the drapes and wept
The gate was taken prisoner
By a chain link fence.

www.ingramcontent.com/pod-product-compliance
Lightning Source LLC
Chambersburg PA
CBHW021132020426
42331CB00005B/728